The Missions of California

Mission Santa Inés

Jacqueline Ching

The Rosen Publishing Group's
PowerKids Press™
New York

For my mother, Vivien Kiang Ching

Published in 2000, 2003 by The Rosen Publishing Group, Inc.
29 East 21st Street, New York, NY 10010

Revised Edition 2003

Book Design: Danielle Primiceri

Layout Design: Maria Melendez

Photo Credits and Photo Illustrations: pp. 1, 8, 9, 12, 23, 24, 25, 26, 27, 35, 44, 47, 48, 49, 50, 51 © Christina Taccone; pp. 4, 16, 17, 18, 19, 20, 21, 34, 38, 39, 43 © Michael K. Ward; p. 6 © Seaver Center for Western History Research, L.A. County Museum of Natural History; p. 10 © Archive Photos; pp. 15, 36 © The Granger Collection, New York; p. 22 © Ralph A. Clevenger/Corbis; pp. 25, 50 © Shirley Jordan 1995 Santa Inés; p. 29 © Ed Young/Corbis; pp. 31, 37, 45 © SuperStock; p. 46 © ART on FILE/Corbis; pp. 52, 57 by Christine Innamorato; pp. 6, 19, 28, 30, 32, 38 © Tim Hall.

Editorial Consultant Coordinator: Karen Fontanetta, M.A., Curator, Mission San Miguel Arcángel
Historical Photo Consultants: Thomas L. Davis, M.Div., M.A., and Michael K. Ward, M.A.

Ching, Jacqueline.
  Mission Santa Inés / by Jacqueline Ching.
    p. cm. — (The missions of California)
  Includes bibliographical references (p. 62) and index.
  Summary: Discusses the founding, building, and operation of the Spanish Mission Santa Inés and its role in California history.
    ISBN: 0-8239-5894-9 (lib. bdg.)
    1. Santa Inés Mission (Solvang, Calif.) —History Juvenile literature. 2. Spanish mission buildings—California—Solvang Region—History Juvenile literature. 3. Franciscans—California—Solvang Region—History Juvenile literature. 4. Chumash Indians—Missions—California—Solvang Region—History Juvenile literature. 5. California—History—To 1846 Juvenile literature. [1. Santa Inés Mission (Solvang, Calif.) —History. 2. Missions—California. 3. Indians of North America—Missions—California. 4. California—History—To 1846.]
  I. Title. II. Series.
    F869.S487 C45 1999
    979.4'91—dc21
                                                   99.21540
                                                   CIP

Contents

The Spanish in California

In the 1500s, the Spanish explored a vast area of the Americas. Bold explorers came looking for new riches or a new way of life and met the American Indians who were native to this land. The Spanish empire in the Americas spread from the southwest desert of North America to the Andes Mountains in South America. This empire was called New Spain. Everywhere the Spanish colonists went, they spread Spanish culture and the Christian religion.

In 1542, the Spanish claimed California. This was the last territory on the borders of the empire to become part of New Spain. At the time, "California" consisted of what is now California and the Baja Peninsula of Mexico. It was divided into two parts, Alta, or upper, California and Baja, or lower, California.

By 1768, however, Spain still had not built any settlements in Alta California. There were many reasons the Spaniards had not built communities there. Alta California was a large unknown territory, and until this time no settlers had shown any interest in it.

Spain soon learned that the Russians wanted to settle in Alta California. Russian explorers and fur traders had established colonies in Alaska and were moving farther south to hunt sea otters. The lands of Alta California were also rich, fertile, and near the sea. It was a perfect place to build towns and harbors for ships. Whoever controlled the coast could control trade routes across the Pacific Ocean. The Spanish government was afraid to lose this important territory to the Russians.

It was decided that a chain of missions would be set up along the coast of Alta California. Spanish friars would settle there, with soldiers nearby to protect them. The Spaniards had already built missions

◀ *Spanish friars traveled to Alta California to help establish the mission system there.*

outside of Alta California and thought that it was a good way to begin settling a territory.

The Mission Community

In the eyes of the missionaries, however, the main goal of the missions was to convert the local American Indians to Christianity. The Spanish king and church leaders believed it was their God-given duty to convert the American Indians, as well as to protect them. Once converted, the American Indians were supposed to do Christian work by building mission structures and raising crops and livestock.

The Spaniards built 21 missions along the coast of California over a period of 54 years. Mission San Diego de Alcalá, the first mission, was founded in 1769. Mission San Francisco de Solano, the last mission, was founded in 1823. In the end, the missions were about a day's ride apart from each other on the best farming lands and formed a chain up the California coast. Small towns eventually grew near or around them. The mission communities traded crops, cattle, and other goods with the people in the towns.

▲
The lives of the Indians changed drastically with the arrival of the Spanish.

Each mission converted hundreds of American Indians. These neophytes, as the newly converted were called, had to obey the missionary in charge. He told them what to do and how to live. The missionaries thought that once the American Indians had learned the Christian way of life and worship, the land could be returned to them. Unfortunately, it didn't turn out that way. The lives of the American Indians would never be the same again after the mission system.

○ San Francisco Solano
○ San Rafael Arcángel
○ San Francisco de Asís
○ San José
○ Santa Clara de Asís
○ Santa Cruz
○ San Juan Bautista
○ San Carlos Borromeo de Carmelo
○ Nuestra Señora de la Soledad

○ San Antonio de Padua
○ San Miguel Arcángel

○ San Luis Obispo de Tolosa

○ La Purísima Concepción
○ Santa Inés
○ Santa Bárbara
○ San Buenaventura

○ San Fernando Rey de España
○ San Gabriel Arcángel

○ San Juan Capistrano

○ San Luis Rey de Francia

○ San Diego de Alcalá

From San Francisco de Solano to San Diego de Alcalá, 21 missions lined the coast of Alta California.

Founding Mission Santa Inés

There were already 18 missions in California when the mission friars asked the Spanish government for a new one. Most of the missions were just 30 miles (48.3 km) apart on El Camino Real, the main road connecting them. Two of the missions, Santa Bárbara and La Purísima Concepción were too far apart. Many Indian families lived in between them. The friars of New Spain wanted to build a mission closer to these families. They wanted to convert the Indians to Christianity.

Fray Estévan Tápis, president of the missions since 1803, went in search of a good location for the new mission. He chose a place on a high knoll next to the Santa Ynez River. It was a beautiful place, surrounded by oak-covered mountains. The American Indians called it Alajulapa, meaning "corner." Here, the land supplied many trees for lumber, good soil for growing crops, and plenty of fresh water for drinking. Everything the missionaries needed for survival was right there.

On September 17, 1804, Mission Santa Inés became the 19th mission in California. Fray Tápis celebrated the first Mass with the help of Frays Marcelino Ciprés, José Antonio

◄ *One of the bell posts along El Camino Real*

A front view of Mission Santa Inés ▶

▲
Mission Santa Inés was dedicated to Saint Agnes.

Calzada, and José Romualdo Gutierrez. They built a shelter out of brushwood for the founding ceremonies. The friars baptized 27 Indian children on that day.

Most missions were dedicated to saints of the Catholic Church. This one was dedicated to Saint Agnes, a Christian martyr. Saint Agnes lived in fourth-century Rome. She was put to death at the age of 13 because she refused to give up her Christian faith. Legend holds that she restored the sight of a blind man by praying. She is still one of the most popular Christian saints.

The families of the 27 baptized children became members of the mission. By the end of the first year, 277 other American Indians had come to Mission Santa Inés from overcrowded missions nearby. A total of 570 Indians were living at Mission Santa Inés.

Although Mission Santa Inés was smaller than the other missions, it was a major producer of goods. The friars taught the neophytes many trades, and the Indians continued to put their own skills to use.

The community of friars and neophytes grew many crops, including wheat, barley, corn, and beans. The mission's livestock increased. This included cattle, sheep, horses, mules, and pigs. The mission warehouse was filled with the many kinds of goods they made, including animal hides, tallow for candles and soap, cloth woven from wool, and dairy products.

The neophytes learned to make beautiful saddles decorated with silver. Thanks to the skill of the neophytes, the mission became known for its leather and metal products.

The Founding Fathers

The first Spanish friars to build missions in the American southwest were the Jesuits. In 1767, however, the government of Spain removed them in favor of the Franciscans. The Jesuits, Franciscans, and Dominicans are religious orders, or groups, of the Roman Catholic Church. Each one is devoted to missionary work.

Spain's interest in settling Alta California came the year after the Jesuits had to stop their missionary work in the Americas. It was the Franciscans who built the missions in Alta California.

Fray Junípero Serra

In 1769, Fray Junípero Serra, along with the military leader Captain Gaspar de Portola, led the Franciscan expedition into Alta California. Born in Majorca, Spain, in 1713, Serra joined the Franciscan order at age 16. He became a professor and a preacher, but he always hoped to do missionary work. At age 36, he got his chance to go to New Spain. In 1768, when the Franciscans took over, Fray Serra became the first president of the missions in Baja California.

The following year, Fray Serra became the first president of the missions in Alta California. The first mission he founded was Mission San Diego de Alcalá. The ride from Loreto in Baja California to San Diego was 750 miles (1,207 km). In spite of having an infected leg, Fray Serra made the entire journey. There was no question that Fray Serra was a man unparalleled in his devotion to missionary work.

Frays Tápis, Calzada, and Gutierrez

Santa Inés was the only mission founded by Fray Tápis. He was

◀ *Fray Junípero Serra was known as the father of the California missions.*

known for his musical talents and for teaching the neophytes to sing and play instruments that were new to them. As president of the missions, he did not stay to run the affairs of Mission Santa Inés. It was Fray Calzada and Fray Gutierrez who took on this task as the mission's first resident friars.

After Fray Calzada died in 1814, Mission Santa Inés came under the guidance of 10 more friars over the years. Some of them died and were buried in the church at the mission.

Beliefs of the Founding Fathers

The Spanish missionaries' goal was to convert the American Indians to Christianity. They believed that they were saving the souls of the Indians by making them members of the Catholic Church. The friars also believed that they were protecting the Indians by converting them to Christianity. This was because as Christians, the Indians would become full citizens of the Spanish empire and would therefore be entitled to own land. The friars truly wanted to help the American Indians. Unfortunately, their good intentions did not end up helping the Indians, but hurting them. The mission system forced many California Indians to give up their way of life and cultural traditions that they had known for generations.

The Spanish friars felt that they were responsible for both the physical and spiritual well-being of the American Indians. ▶

The American Indians

The Chumash Tribe

When the Spaniards first arrived in Alta California, many American Indian tribes were already living there. There were over 100 different Indian groups, each with its own land and identity, and its own language or dialect. The American Indians who lived on lands surrounding Mission Santa Inés belonged to the Chumash tribe.

The Chumash tribe once lived all along the Southern California coastline. The Chumash Indians called themselves the First People. They were generally a nonviolent people who loved music and made it a part of their everyday lives. They sang songs for celebrations, like the birth of a baby, and for healing, hunting, warfare, and harvesting. Their musical instruments included rattles made from turtle shells, whistles made from wood and the bones of birds, and string instruments similar to the hunting bow.

Chumash Indians valued their possessions. They used beads made out of shells as money to buy such things as cloth, meat, or deer skins.

Some Indian hunters wore deer skins. ▶

Before the Spanish arrived, many Native Americans lived in villages. ▶

The Chumash were skilled craftspeople. They made fine baskets for storage, offerings, and gifts. Other tribes often made blankets from animal fur, but the Chumash Indians were known to weave feathers into the beautiful blankets that they made. The Chumash Indians would later turn their skills into great success for Mission Santa Inés.

▲
The Chumash Indians built dome-shaped houses.

Chumash Housing

The Chumash Indians built dome-shaped houses. These were usually 12 (3.7 m) to 20 feet (6.1 m) long. Some were single-family homes, while others housed three or four families, sometimes up to 50 people. Sycamore poles or willow branches were used as frames for these houses, and whale ribs were used to build the doorways.

Canoes were as important to the coastal Chumash as horses were to the Plains Indians. The Chumash word for canoe was *tomol*. They built their canoes from wood they brought down from the mountains. These canoes, which were used mostly for fishing, could hold 12 to 20 people. For the Chumash Indians, who lived on the coast, fish was an important food.

▲

The Indians fished from canoes or from the shore with long spears.

Hunting and Gathering

In addition to catching fish, the Indians hunted game and gathered berries, seeds, and nuts. Hunting and gathering had always been how the American Indians survived, but these methods did not always provide a steady source of food. Sometimes the Indians would go

A Chumash Indian gravesite

hungry. The Indians did not farm the land or raise cattle. They did not cut down forests or kill off whole animal populations. Instead, they lived in harmony with nature, eating whatever was available in the wild.

The only gardening done by the California Indians was growing tobacco. They smoked, chewed, and ate the tobacco. It was also used by the shamans, medicine men believed to have special powers, in their ceremonies to cure the sick.

Ceremonial Life

Ceremonies played an important part in the lives of the American Indians. As hunter-gatherers, the Chumash lived close to nature, so their ceremonies marked important times of the year like harvest time, the winter solstice, and the return of spring.

They used amulets, made from painted stones, for luck in fishing and hunting trips. These stones were also used by the shamans.

The shaman was an important person in an Indian tribe because he communicated between humans and the spirit world. The shamans and craftsmen made up the upper class of the Chumash tribe.

Some Indian tribes cremated their dead, but the Chumash had burials. In May 1997, an intact Chumash grave was found at Avila Beach in San Luis Obispo. Clay bowls, whistles, and smoking pipes were found nearby.

The Chumash Indians also drew pictographs, or paintings, on the walls of caves. The pictographs told the stories of their way of life. The earliest paintings were black. Later, they were red, and still later, they were made with several colors. The colors were made from different rocks and minerals. For example, charcoal was used to make black paint, and the mineral hematite made red. These pictographs can still be seen in the Santa Ynez Mountains.

Chumash Indians often drew pictures on the walls of caves. ▶

Building the Mission

Roof tiles at the mission

Immediately after the founding of Mission Santa Inés, the community set to work on the permanent buildings. By the end of March 1804, they had built the first wing of the mission, a row of adobe buildings with thatched roofs. Adobe, which was used throughout the mission buildings, is sundried brick made of soil, water, and straw. In this first wing was the sacristy, where holy objects were kept, a granary, where grain was stored, the church, and living space for Frays Calzada and Gutierrez.

Two more wings were built by 1806, and other buildings followed as needed. Eighty adobe huts with doors and windows were built for the Indian families in 1812. It was in December of that year that a terrible earthquake shook Southern California, damaging many of the missions.

The Mission Church

The earthquake of 1812 destroyed the first church at Mission Santa Inés and caused serious damage to the other buildings, but the friars were determined to rebuild. By 1813, a

◄ *A view of the mission's many arches.*

◄ *After the earthquake of 1812, a second, larger church was built. It can still be seen today.*

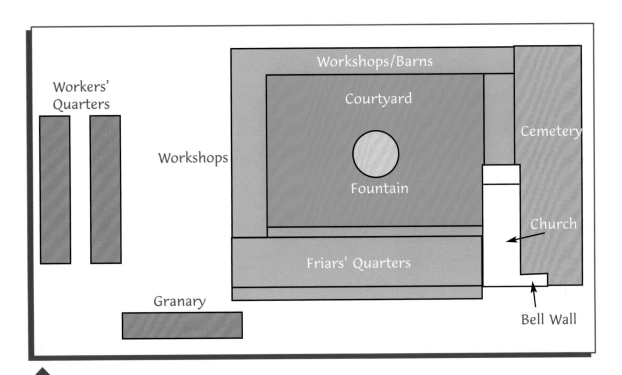

The general layout of Mission Santa Inés.

monjerío, or living quarters, for unmarried girls, was completed, as was a granary, which was used as a temporary place of worship. Work on the new church would not begin until the next year.

On July 4, 1817, the mission community celebrated the completion of the new church. The three bells in the tower rang on that day. It had taken two years just to finish the outside of the church. The adobe walls were built five

◀ *The mission walls were made of adobe.*

24

▲
The interior of the mission as decorated by the neophytes.

(1.5 m) to six feet (1.8 m) thick to make the church as sturdy as possible. Beams were made of heavy pine from nearby Figueroa Mountain. Above the sanctuary, the ceiling was made of painted wood.

Interior Design

The insides of the buildings were decorated with paints made in the age-old ways of the Chumash Indians. They used the same rocks and minerals they had used to make paint for their pictographs. They also added herbs, roots, and berries to make new colors. These were used to paint decorations of vines, baskets, vases, and even marble.

The floors of the church were built of Indian-made tiles. Some of the floor tiles still have the footprints of children and animals in them. It seems that they had stepped on the tiles while the tiles were still drying!

▲
The skilled Chumash Indians created many beautiful designs.

25

The floor tiles at Mission Santa Inés still remain in place today.

General Features of the Mission

The rest of Mission Santa Inés was built as a quadrangle, a four-sided enclosure around which stood the mission buildings. This followed the traditional design of other missions. Next to the church and cemetery were the friars' rooms, offices, living and guest rooms, and a *monjerío*. These stood on one side of a square. Workshops, barns, stables, and warehouses formed the other sides of the square.

All the members of the mission community would meet in the center of the square where a fountain stood. It was here that they celebrated festivals, played games, sang songs, and danced.

A brick building stood in front of the mission. This was used for bathing and washing. On one side were the gardens and orchards, and on the other were the huts and tiled houses where the Indian families lived.

The mission got its water supply from the mountains. First the community dug ditches, then they lined them

The fountain lies in the center of the mission.

26

with waterproof pipes. The pipes carried water from the mountains to the mission.

From the day the new church was finished, luck seemed to be on the side of Mission Santa Inés. Its flocks and herds grew quickly.

The mission was located in such a beautiful valley that it was called "The Hidden Gem of the Missions." Even so, Mission Santa Inés had few visitors. This was because it was far away from the main roads and difficult to reach. For this reason whenever visitors came, the friars and neophytes would give them a warm welcome. Someone would ring the church bell to signal to the community that a visitor was approaching. There were special signals to let the community know if the visitor was a friar, an American Indian, or a European settler. Everyone at the mission would gather at the door to greet the visitor.

Visitors were announced by the ringing of bells.

◀ *The front door of Mission Santa Inés.*

27

Daily Life at the Mission

Life for the neophytes at Mission Santa Inés was like that of the other missions. At dawn the church bells woke them and called everyone to church. After morning prayers and Mass, they sat down to breakfast. Breakfast was usually *atole*, a porridge made of corn, which was always served at mealtimes. Breakfast was followed by morning chores.

The men went to work in the fields or in a workshop. The women and girls began their weaving or other chores. The boys started their lessons with the friars or did chores of their own.

The friars taught the male neophytes to read and write, not only in Spanish, but in Latin, too. This was thought to be important, mainly so that the Indians could understand the Bible.

At noon the bells interrupted everyone's work for the midday meal. This was usually *pozole*, cornmeal eaten with beans, vegetables, or meat. Then, the neophytes took a *siesta*, an afternoon nap, until 2:00 P.M. before starting work again.

The men spent the rest of the day working in the fields. They herded the cattle, horses, and sheep. When harvest season was over, they made

◀ *The Indians were taught to work in new ways.*

The mission garden is in a courtyard surrounded by the friars' quarters, workshops, and church. ▶

Indian women cooked meals for the mission community.

adobe bricks or tiles, which would be used for new buildings.

Inside the *monjerío*, the women weaved. They produced all of the cloth used at the mission, including blankets, sheets, tablecloths, towels, and napkins.

Free Time

At sundown the bells ended the workday, and the evening meal was prepared. Afterward there was time for games, gambling, and other pastimes before the bells rang for evening prayers.

One of the games the Chumash Indians played was like an early version of hockey. It was played on a large open field with two teams. Each team used sticks to get a small wooden ball through the other team's goal post. The team with the most goals won.

No one worked on Sundays or holidays. On these days, the neophytes were free to do what they liked after the morning Mass and afternoon prayers. Sometimes they were even allowed to visit their native villages if they wished.

The mission was dedicated to Saint Agnes, so the "Dia de Santa

▲

The Chumash Indians loved to play games.

Inés," or Saint Agnes's Feast Day, was one of the most important festivals at the mission. It was celebrated with horse races and bullfights on a large open square.

The lives of American Indian boys and girls at the missions were very different. At around age 11, the girls had to leave their mothers and live at the *monjerío*. They worked in the *monjerío*, too. Once they finished their work, they were allowed to visit their families. They were locked in at night. Girls had to live at the *monjerío* under strict supervision until they were married.

The neophyte boys were not locked in at night or forced to stay in during the day. The friars trained the boys to become bell ringers, sing in the choir, or play the violin.

Some friars scolded Indians for not working hard enough or for breaking the rules.

A New Way of Life

The American Indians lived a life of order at the missions, but it was very different from the life they once knew. When the missionaries first came to them, the American Indians could not foresee that they would lose their freedom, be forced to give up their way of life, and be kept inside the missions.

Many of the neophytes tried to run away from the missions, but the soldiers would go after them and bring them back. Other neophytes remained willingly at the missions.

The missions did, however, try to give the neophytes protection from traders and other settlers who, in their search for gold and silver, had little regard for the lives of the American Indians.

The friars wanted to protect the American Indians, but they were simply unable to. The cruelty of other European settlers and the diseases that they brought with them would prove too strong. Furthermore, the friars did not understand that the American Indians deserved to live the way they always had. At that time in history, the Spanish did not understand that the American Indians' culture was just as important and as valuable as their own. Today we might look at the treatment of the California Indians under the mission system as a great injustice that violated their civil rights. Indeed, as with many systems, the mission system had both strengths and weaknesses. It allowed two very different cultures to interact and, in many cases, to coexist in successful, productive communities. However, it also caused one people to lose much of its independence and cultural identity.

Troubled Times

Nature's Trials

On December 21, 1812, an earthquake struck Mission Santa Inés, causing much damage. One end of the church collapsed and many of the houses near the church were destroyed. The two earthquake tremors, which were 15 minutes apart, ruined all the roofs and cracked many of the walls. In other words, it only took 15 minutes to destroy eight years of hard work.

Indian Rebellion

The damage done by the earthquake, however, paled in comparison to the damage done by fighting and disease. In February 1824, an Indian rebellion swept Missions Santa Inés and La Purísima Concepción, as well as others in the Santa Barbara area. It was the most successful rebellion of neophytes in the history of the missions.

The trouble had been brewing since the start of Mexico's war for independence from Spain in 1810. Spain spent so much of its resources fighting this war that it could no longer support the missions. As a result, the mission soldiers did not

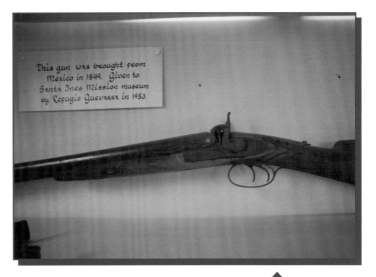

A gun used in Mexico's war for independence

The Native Americans revolted against the Spanish.

35

▲

This painting depicts a scene from Mexico's war for independence from Spain.

receive their wages and supplies regularly.

The soldiers began to depend on the missions for food, clothing, and other supplies. The neophytes had to work harder and harder, without pay to support the soldiers. To make matters worse, the soldiers mistreated the Indians. Of course, this made the Chumash Indians very angry.

When a comet appeared in the sky in December 1823, the Chumash saw this as a sign from their god Chupu that things would soon change. Then in February, a neophyte from Mission La Purísima Concepción was visiting a relative at Mission Santa Inés and was whipped by a Spanish soldier there. This was the last straw for the Chumash. A signal was given and more than a thousand Indians attacked Mission Santa Inés with bows and arrows. Although they were angry at the soldiers and not the friars, who had been kind to them, several friars were wounded in the course of the fighting.

In the revolt against the Santa Inés soldiers, two American Indians were killed, several buildings were set on fire, and all of the friars were held hostage.

In 1824, more than a thousand Indians attacked Mission Santa Inés.

The fighting at Mission Santa Inés continued until the next day. A few soldiers from Santa Bárbara soon arrived, and the Indian rebels fled to Mission La Purísima Concepción. They joined rebel Indians there and took over that mission. The Indians took the friars and the families of the soldiers hostage. Then they waited for a battle.

Almost a month passed, and then more than a hundred Mexican soldiers arrived at Mission La Purísima Concepción. The battle lasted only three hours. By the end of the fighting one soldier and 16 Indians were dead.

Many Indians became sick and died from European diseases.

Disease Strikes the Indians

Although many Indians died at the hands of soldiers, many more died from diseases brought by European settlers. Without knowing it, the Spaniards carried diseases with them from Europe to the Americas. These diseases, such as measles, smallpox, flu, and the common cold, did not always kill Europeans, but they did kill many American Indians.

▲

With secularization, many Indians went back to their villages.

Their bodies were not immune or prepared to fight these new diseases. The effect was tragic. The American Indian population rapidly declined.

Secularization

Another source of trouble for the missions came from the Mexican government. In 1821, Mexico won its war for independence from Spain, and Alta California became part of Mexico. This had a disastrous effect on the California missions.

In 1834, the Mexican government passed a law called the Act of Secularization. Secularization meant taking financial control of the missions away from the Catholic Church. The missions would no longer be used by missionaries to convert American Indians to Christianity. Instead the missions would only be used to preserve the faith of Christianity.

The missions were turned into parishes and the Indians were free to leave. One half of the land was to be divided among the American Indians and the other half was to be used for agriculture and other common needs. Instead, however, the land was illegally given or sold to Mexican ranchers. Many American Indians did not understand the concept of land ownership. They thought the land should be for everybody. To them, owning a piece of land was as ridiculous as owning a piece of sky!

Many Indians went back to their mountain villages or went to work at ranches for little more than room and board. Other Indians remained behind because they had nowhere else to go. Their villages no longer existed. Their own ways of hunting and gathering were lost. Their special language and ceremonial rituals were forgotten. Without their own culture, many American Indians did not have the means to live better lives in freedom than they had lived at the missions.

After secularization, the horses belonging to the mission were given to the soldiers. Soon the number of cattle decreased. Things went from bad to worse until the friars and the Indians who were left had barely enough food to live on. Sometimes the friars of Mission Santa Inés had to hunt for animal meat themselves. By 1840, only 180 Indians were left at the mission. The community that the friars and neophytes had built was falling apart.

For a long time, there were rumors that the mission would be sold, and finally, in 1846, these rumors became truth. Mission Santa Inés was sold for $7,000 to two Mexican settlers, José Covarrubias and Joaquin Carrillo. The well-organized community life of the mission was gone forever.

Stories and Legends

The Story of Pasquala

There is a story that in 1824, a young Indian girl named Pasquala saved Mission Santa Inés from total destruction. She did this by warning Fray Uría that her people were planning a rebellion.

Her people were the Yokut Indians, who lived northeast of the area controlled by the peaceful Chumash. The Yokut Indians were not so peaceful. They were ready to go to war when they thought it necessary.

When Pasquala's family became Christian at Mission Santa Inés, the Yokut Indians were very angry. They killed her father while he was working in the mission vineyards and kidnapped Pasquala and her mother. They were brought to a ranch where her mother later died.

When Pasquala heard about the Yokuts' plan to attack, she escaped the ranch and walked for days through the rocky hills and valleys to reach the mission. When she reached it, she shouted to Fray Uría, "Padre! War! War!" The friar prepared the soldiers for the oncoming attack.

The difficult journey to the mission was too much for Pasquala. She became sick and died. Fray Uría was so sad that he decided to bury her in the church, even though Indians were usually buried elsewhere.

The Legend of the Waterfall

An American Indian legend of the Santa Ynez Valley tells the story of a waterfall the Chumash Indians named Nojoqui. It goes back many years to a time when a drought brought fear and suffering to their people. To calm the Great Spirit, the Indians, led by their chief, went to

The young Indian girl Pasquala ▶

PADRE PADRE ---WAR WAR

afternoon Feb. 21, 1824, a senseless ... beloved Mission that nig[h]
...tructive raid was made on this ...

▲

Pasquala warned Fray Uría that her tribe was preparing an attack.

the mouth of a canyon. There, the chief left his people and went alone into the darkness of the canyon.

As he walked farther into the canyon, he had a vision. A sparkling figure appeared and pointed toward a beautiful waterfall. The figure said, "See, this is yours." The chief quickly returned to his people and brought them to the rushing water. The next day, the Indians woke up to rain. The drought was over! For years afterward, and into the mission days, they would go to Nojoqui Falls and throw a token of thanks into the waterfall for having saved their people.

The Pirate Joseph Chapman

Mission Santa Inés once employed Joseph Chapman, a man who had come to the California coast as a pirate! Joseph Chapman led a life of adventure. He worked aboard the ship of French pirate Hippolyte de Bouchard. A constant menace in the Pacific Ocean, Bouchard attacked Spanish ships and raided Spanish ports from the Philippines to Hawaii.

In 1818, Bouchard and his crew sailed to Alta California to raid the Spanish settlements there. Among his crew was Joseph Chapman. After plundering a ranch near Santa Barbara, Chapman and others were captured and imprisoned.

After his release, Chapman became a new man. He was baptized as a Catholic and married into a respectable family. Chapman and his wife moved to Santa Inés, where he was hired as a handyman. The mission benefited from his skill in planting vineyards and in building. In 1821, Chapman built the mission's fulling mill, which was used to treat wool so that it was less scratchy.

A former pirate once worked at Mission Santa Inés. ▶

The Modern-Day Mission

Today Mission Santa Inés is one of the best preserved Spanish missions in the United States. The low, flat lands on which its orchards grew are now fields of wheat. You can still find the pipes that the neophytes laid down so that the mission could receive water from the mountains.

▲ *Today many people are baptized and married at Mission Santa Inés.*

Nearby, on a Chumash reservation, descendants of the mission's neophytes carry on the job of rediscovering and preserving their culture.

Today, about 1,300 families belong to the Santa Inés parish. The church still performs baptisms, funerals, and

◄ *A view through the mission's arches*

◄ *The bell tower at Mission Santa Inés*

▲

The altar at the church

other ceremonies. This active parish church continues to serve the community.

Some of the buildings that the friars and neophytes built still stand. There is the adobe church, the *monjerío*, and the American Indian village. Inside the buildings, you can see examples of the Indians' fine arts and crafts. The dyes made by the Chumash Indians were so pure that some of the decorations inside the church still show their original colors.

In 1904, Fray Alexander Buckler started a 20-year restoration project. The original mission was so large, he decided to restore only about one-fourth of the original mission quadrangle.

Today, these restored buildings are in such excellent condition that the National Landmark Committee has made Mission Santa Inés a national landmark. It will be preserved for future generations to visit, so they can learn about the lives of the friars and neophytes of the California missions.

This is a view of the mission's fountain and garden. (inset) A restored stone wall at Mission Santa Inés is shown here. ▶

Fray Serra's vestment ▶

Metal objects used at the mission from 1810-1820
▼

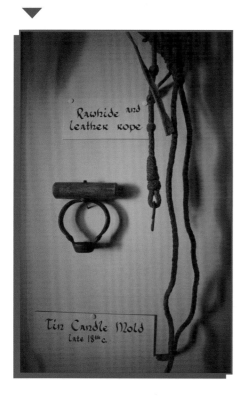

◀ *The church of Mission Santa Inés contains many beautiful statues.*

Make Your Own Model Mission Santa Inés

To make your own model of the Santa Inés mission, you will need:

wire mesh	miniature bell
scissors	red paint
ruler	paintbrush
wire	foamcore base
glue	greenery

Directions

Step 1. Cut out eight pieces of wire mesh that are 12″ x 2″ (30.5 cm x 5 cm) to form the base and the roof of the mission.

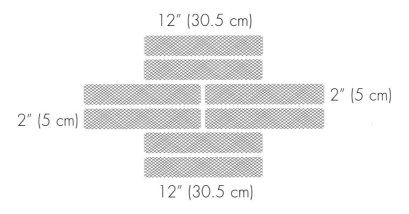

Adult supervision is suggested.

Step 2. Use the wire to sew together four of the mesh pieces into a flat square. Repeat this step to form another square.

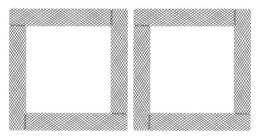

Step 3. Cut out two pieces of mesh to measure 12" x 3" (30.5 cm x 7.6 cm). These will form the sides of the mission.

12" (30.5 cm)

3" (7.6 cm)

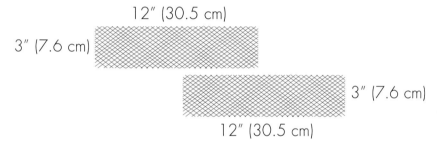

3" (7.6 cm)

12" (30.5 cm)

Step 4. Sew one of the 12" x 3" (30.5 cm x 7.6 cm) mesh rectangles perpendicular to one 12" (30.5 cm) side of the base. Attach the other 12" x 3" (30.5 cm x 7.6 cm) mesh rectangle to the opposite side.

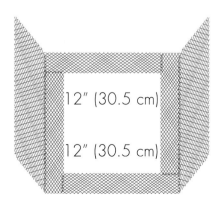

12" (30.5 cm)

12" (30.5 cm)

53

Step 5. Cut out eight pieces of mesh that are 3" x 2" (7.6 cm x 5 cm). Bend the edges of each piece to make them look like 3" (7.6 cm) columns.

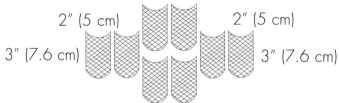

2" (5 cm)   2" (5 cm)

3" (7.6 cm)   3" (7.6 cm)

Step 6. Attach one of the columns to the left side of the mission front. Attach another column 6" (15.2 cm) from the other side. Attach two more columns equal distance from each other.

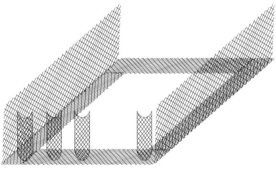

Step 7. On the back of the mission, attach the other four columns an equal distance from each other.

Step 8. Cut out a 3" x 4" (7.6 cm x 10.1 cm) piece of mesh. This will be the front of the church.

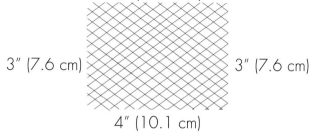

4" (10.1 cm)

3" (7.6 cm) 3" (7.6 cm)

4" (10.1 cm)

Step 9. Cut out the bell wall from the wire mesh. This shape should be about 3" x 6" (7.6 cm x 15.2 cm). Decorate the top of the bell wall and glue a wire cross on top.

6" (15.2 cm)

3" (7.6 cm)

Step 10. Attach the church front and the bell wall to the right side of the mission base. The bell wall should be the farthest to the right. Attach a miniature bell to the bell wall with wire.

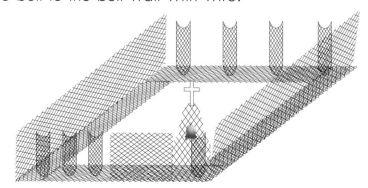

Step 11. Using wire, sew the pieces of the roof onto the mission.

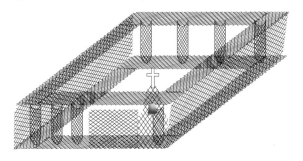

Step 12. Paint the roof red. Let dry.

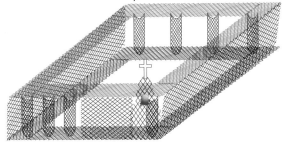

Step 13. To make the workshops, cut out two mesh pieces that are 2″ x 2″ (5 cm x 5 cm) and four pieces that are 2″ x 6″ (5 cm x 15.2 cm).

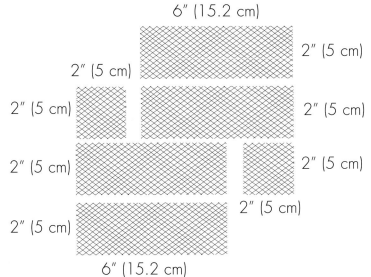

6″ (15.2 cm)

2″ (5 cm)

2″ (5 cm)

2″ (5 cm)

2″ (5 cm)

2″ (5 cm)

2″ (5 cm)

2″ (5 cm)

2″ (5 cm)

6″ (15.2 cm)

Step 14. Use wire to sew these pieces into a box shape.

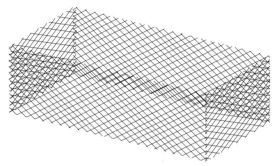

Step 15. Place all buildings on foamcore base. Decorate the mission with flowers and trees as you want it to look.

*Use the above mission as a reference for building your mission.

Important Dates in Mission History

1492	Christopher Columbus reaches the West Indies
1542	Cabrillo's expedition to California
1602	Sebastián Vizcaíno sails to California
1713	Fray Junípero Serra is born
1769	Founding of San Diego de Alcalá
1770	Founding of San Carlos Borromeo de Carmelo
1771	Founding of San Antonio de Padua and San Gabriel Arcángel
1772	Founding of San Luis Obispo de Tolosa
1775–76	Founding of San Juan Capistrano
1776	Founding of San Francisco de Asís
1776	Declaration of Independence is signed
1777	Founding of Santa Clara de Asís
1782	Founding of San Buenaventura
1784	Fray Serra dies
1786	Founding of Santa Bárbara
1787	Founding of La Purísima Concepción
1791	Founding of Santa Cruz and Nuestra Señora de la Soledad
1797	Founding of San José, San Juan Bautista, San Miguel Arcángel, and San Fernando Rey de España
1798	Founding of San Luis Rey de Francia
1804	**Founding of Santa Inés**
1817	Founding of San Rafael Arcángel
1823	Founding of San Francisco Solano
1848	Gold found in northern California
1850	California becomes the 31st state

Glossary

adobe (uh-DOH-bee) Brick made from dried mud and straw.

Alta California (AL-tuh ka-luh-FOR-nyuh) The area where the Spanish settled missions, today known as the state of California.

amulet (AM-yoo-let) Something worn to bring good luck or to keep away bad luck.

citizen (SIH-tih-zen) A person who is born in or has the legal right to live in a certain country.

colonists (KAH-luh-nists) People who settle in a new land.

convert (kon-VERT) To cause someone to change beliefs or religions.

drought (DROWT) A long period of dry weather, with little or no rain.

empire (EM-pyr) A large area under one ruler.

Franciscan (fran-SIS-kan) Friars belonging to the Franciscan order, a part of the Catholic Church started by Saint Francis in 1209.

friar (FRY-ur) A brother in a communal religious order. Friars can also be priests.

granary (GRA-nah-ree) A windowless building used for storing grain.

hostage (HOS-tij) A person who is held as a prisoner until some demand is agreed to.

martyr (MAR-ter) A person who is put to death or made to suffer because of his religious beliefs.

Mass (MASS) The main religious ceremony of some churches, such as the Catholic Church.

missionary (MIH-shun-ayr-ee) A person who teaches his or her religion to people with different religious beliefs.

neophyte (NEE-oh-fyt) A person who has converted to another religion.

padre (PAH-dray) The Spanish word for father or priest.

parish (PAR-ish) An area with its own church and minister or priest.

plundering (PLUN-der-ing) Robbing by force.

sanctuary (SANGK-choo-ayr-ee) The most holy place in a church.

secularization (sehk-yoo-luh-rih-ZAY-shun) A process by which the mission lands were made to be nonreligious.

settlement (SEH-tul-ment) A small village or group of houses.

thatch (THACH) Tule or reeds used to build a roof or covering.

Pronunciation Guide

atole (ah-TOL-ay)

Chumash (CHOO-mahsh)

convento (kam-BEN-toh)

El Camino Real (El kah-MEE-no RAY-al)

fray (FRAY)

monjerío (mohn-hay-REE-oh)

pozole (poh-ZOHL-ay)

pueblos (PWAY-blohs)

siesta (see-EHS-tah)

tomol (TOH-mul)

Resources

To learn more about the California missions, check out these books, Web sites, and video:

Books:

Genet, Donna. *Father Junípero Serra: Founder of the California Missions.* Springfield, NJ: Enslow Publishers, 1996.

Van Steenwyk, Elizabeth. *The California Missions.* Newburyport, MA: Franklin Watts, 1998.

Web Sites:

Due to the changing nature of Internet links, PowerKids Press has developed an online list of Web sites related to the subject of this book. This site is updated regularly. Please use this link to access the list: www.powerkidslinks.com/moca/santines/

Video:

Missions of California: Father Junípero Serra.
Produced by Chip Taylor Productions
This 11-minute, full-color video features pictures of Fray Serra, detailed maps, and beautiful scenery from many of the missions he founded. It should be available in your library. You can also order the video by calling 1-800-876-CHIP.

Index